31 DAYS TO ELIM

ACKNOWLEDGEMENTS

Proofing by Henry Jaffe
Portman Lodge Limited, hjaffe@portmanlodge.com

Graphics designed by Joe Luk,
Designer and Creative, info@joeluk.co.uk

Unless otherwise stated.
Scripture quotations are taken from
The Holy Bible, New King James Version.
Copyright, Thomas Nelson publishers

Why People Like to Gossip | Psychology Today
Peng, X., Li, Y., Wang, P., Mo, L., & Chen, Q. (2015). Social
Neuroscience, 10, 320-336.

Dictionary.com...
Dictionary.com | Meanings & Definitions of English Words

Meriam Webster's Dictionary
https://www.meriam-webster.com

The New Encyclopaedia of Christian Quotations,
compiled by
Mark Water, John Hunt publishing Ltd, Hampshire, 2000

Billy Age 4
https://bellissimanh.wordpress.com/2012/03/29/your-name-is-safe-in-their-mouth/

Goodreads
https://www.goodreads.com/quotes/tag/gossip

The Guardian
https://www.theguardian.com/world/2019/may/01/have-you-heard-about-the-philippine-mayor-who-banned-Gossip

Psychological facts gossiping
https://www.This study reveals some psychological facts about Gossiping - Gossip mongering | The Economic Times (indiatimes.com)

Christian quotations

George Aitchison

Elaine Roberts has asserted the right as author of this material and it is subject to copyright law. It may not be copied, stored in any system without due acknowledgment of author. ©

WHY THIS BOOK WAS WRITTEN 10

HOW TO USE THIS BOOK 13

WHY 31 DAYS? 16

DEDICATION..19

INTRODUCTION 20

DEFINITIONS 22

ENTER TALEBEARER 23

PROLOGUE   24

DAY 1

LET NO CORRUPT COMMUNICATION PROCEED FROM YOUR MOUTH 25

DAY 2

YOUR MOTHER CAN'T KNIT...28

DAY 3

TRUE, KIND, NECESSARY..32

DAY 4

TOPIC OF JUICY GOSSIP 34

DAY 5

BREAKING CONFIDENCE...36

DAY 6

SLANDER...37

GOSSIP IS ILLEGAL...38

DAY 7

STRAIGHT FROM THE HORSE'S MOUTH 40

DAY 8

WE ARE OUR BROTHERS KEEPER....................................42

DAY 9

WHY ARE YOU SAYING THIS TO ME?..............................46

DAY 10

PERMISSION AND HAPPY 49

DAY 11

FAULT FINDING...52

DAY 12

STOP THEM IN THEIR TRACKS..54

FAST FACTS ABOUT GOSSIP 55

DAY 13

STOP! They are not here...57

DAY 14

LA LA LA I'm not listening 59

DAY 15

CHALLENGE, CHALLENGE, CHALLENGE............................60

DAY 16

EMPATHISE AND SYMPATHISE..62

DAY 17

DEFEND THEIR HONOUR..64

DAY 18

ALWAYS ASSUME CONFIDENTIALITY..66

GOSSIP AS EVIDENCE OF CULTURAL LEARNING 68

DAY 19

NEVER SWEAR 69

DAY 20

SECOND-HAND IS ALWAYS CHEAPER 71

DAY 21

EXIT...73

DAY 22

CHANGE THE SUBJECT 75

DAY 23

I AM NOT IN A POSITION TO SAY..77

DAY 24

CONFESS VULNERABILITIES 79

EFFECTS OF GOSSIP IN THE BRAIN................................81

DAY 25

CAN I REPEAT THIS?..83

DAY 26

PRIVATE LIFE...85

DAY 27

MIND YOUR Ps AND Qs 86

DAY 28

MIND YOUR OWN BUSINESS 88

DAY 29

CAN'T LISTEN - WON'T LISTEN..90

DAY 30

CHOICES 91

DAY 31

WELL DONE!

YOU MADE IT TO DAY 31 93

ABOUT THE AUTHOR 94

31 DAY SERIES..96

MORE TO COME IN THE 31 DAYS SERIES... 97

WHY THIS BOOK WAS WRITTEN

Time is a great teacher; and in 60 years, I have learned many powerful lessons. Lessons that were understood and learned by making mistakes in the first place and then learning not to repeat them.

There was nothing more that Angelina (name changed) and I would enjoy: sitting down and having a good natter about everything and the many people that we both knew. We never engaged in character assassination or reputation annihilation of individuals. We engaged in simple chitchat and the confidential sharing of our opinions about things and people. We also felt comfortable with our private sharing because it was with each other and not with a wider group of people. This made it okay, right?

Wrong!

Boy, how wrong we were.

We both began to feel uncomfortable with our inane chattering and knew that it was wrong. We tried to justify our conversations because they were confined to the two of us.
We felt it was a safe space.

As we became more uncomfortable with our private gossip sessions, one of us came up with a way of challenging each other so that we would stop.

We called it "KO Be Kay." It came from the acronym 'K O B K' – "Kill or Be Killed." We created the acronym. It is not common to anywhere or anyone else.

We figured that when we told each other gossip about somebody we were actually killing the person that we were talking about and we were also killing each other. Killing each other with unnecessary information about others. We were also polluting one another's minds and hearts.

While I was sharing my irrelevant opinion with Angelina, I was polluting her soul and killing her. Likewise, when Angelina was filling my mind with her verbal rubbish, she was killing me too.

So we both agreed to hold each other accountable and challenge one another when our conversations veered into gossip.

As soon as Angelina started talking and it veered into the gossip arena I would say, "KO Be Kay". I was killing gossip from Angelina before she killed me with it. Likewise, if I began talking and it veered into the gossip arena, Angelina would say, "KO Be Kay," so as to kill my gossip and shut it down. I can tell you, it did not take long before the two of us eliminated useless gossip from our conversations. Our conversations from that point on about others were always healthy and uplifting.

To this day, Angelina and I are still the best of friends and we definitely do not discuss the affairs and business of other people.

HOW TO USE THIS BOOK

Use this book as a manual, as a template, as a model. Use it as a reference book to which you may find that you referred to often, for gentle reminders.

Over a lifetime. I have recognised the destructive power of malicious gossip.

Over 30 years ago I prayed a simple and innocent prayer. I prayed, "Dear Lord, please will You use me to eliminate gossip." I felt a kind of silent answer in my heart that said, "You don't know what you are asking."

I thought to myself, "Oh dear, what have I said now?" Nevertheless, I felt a deep conviction in my heart and soul that I wanted to be an instrument that ended gossip, not only in my life, but in the lives of others.

Within the pages of this book, I will be sharing with you the practices I have engaged in, examples/templates you may wish to use to enable and empower you to resist, challenge, shutdown and avoid being the topic of gossip.

I hope you will laugh, be inspired and encouraged as you read on and recognise that others are walking the same corridors of life's university as you and that they are willing to share their pearls of wisdom with you

Reading and applying these 31 life transformative nuggets will augment, amplify, enhance and extend to your life experiences and relationships across all the spheres and spectrums of your life.

Each day will end with a quote from a notable individual who has left their hallmark and legacy of impact upon the world. You are not required to agree with them; simply consider their comments.

Abstaining from gossip will be to your holistic advantage as you will have peace of mind and not be battered with guilt that you have spread, listened to or started gossip. You will have joy in your heart as you speak well of others. The combination of both will be reflected in your general overall health and wellbeing.

You may already not engage in Gossip, and that is fantastic. However, I'm sure you will agree, there is always something new to learn. On the other hand, for you, this may be a weakness. If so, this book is for you to consider the topic and help you improve in this area.

Keep 31 Days to Eliminating Gossip handy as a reference tool for whenever you want a friendly reminder, refresher and top up.

WHY 31 DAYS?

Research has demonstrated that it can take 20-40 days to develop a good habit. The number of days can depend on the personal habits and the individual's commitment to engage in that new habit. Unfortunately, many of us have been victims of knowing what it can be to break a bad habit.

Although this book is called 31 days to Eliminating Gossip, it is not anticipated that it will take you exactly 31 days to accomplish this trait fully. For some it may take less or, for some slightly more.

As you apply each trait to your daily living experience, these 31 nuggets will stimulate your desire for self-improvement.

The passing on of Gossip has become prevalent to the point of almost being out of control, especially with the vast array of social media; whereby in the pressing of the 'forward' button, in less than a nanosecond, reputations and lives can be destroyed.

31 Days to Eliminating Gossip challenges and encourages us to stand out as people of integrity, moral fibre and character for all the right reasons, in that we are not gossips and rumour mongers.

No one is perfect. Nothing we do is perfect. Yet striving for excellence in who we are and seeking to improve our attitudes, thinking, behaviour and character is a must, if we are going to be individuals that leave a legacy of a positive lasting impact.

There is always room for improvement and a better way to do something. There is also a better way to say something and a better way to respond to trials, challenges and tribulations. This book, 31 Days to Eliminating Gossip, will share with you learned wisdom, much of it being personal.

Be informed, equipped and transformed as you seek to become an even better version of you.

You will excel in spirit, mind and body.

Lessons learned in 31 Days will last a lifetime.

DEDICATION

I dedicate this book to
The Rev. Colette Ann Barron.

Colette is a trustee of World Mandate Ministries, an Evangelist and one of my dearest friends.

I dedicate it to Colette because her life epitomises the contents of this book.

In over 20 years of knowing each other, I have never heard Colette contribute to gossip, pass on gossip or listen to negative gossip about anyone. Colette always sees and believes the best in others and speaks highly of them, whether they are present or not.

I can confidently and honestly state that Colette is this book's real-life practical application and example. Thank you Colette, for your shining example to everyone who knows you.

Elaine Roberts

INTRODUCTION

There is talking about people, and *there's talking about people.*

Teachers need to talk to parents about the children they teach to inform them of their child's progress at school. Doctors are required to talk to other consultants about patients to discuss the healthcare of the said patient. The trainee hairdresser and senior hair stylist will talk to each other about a client to discuss their hair requirements, thus enabling the trainee to become an excellent hairdresser. Following an interview, interviewees are discussed amongst the interview panel to decide which one of the applicants is most suitable for the role they have applied for. We recognise there are times when we all need to talk to others about people in relevant and appropriate ways. This book is not designed to stop or interfere with these natural and healthy conversations.

There's Gossip, and *there's Gossip*. There's *good Gossip*, and there is *negative Gossip*. Good Gossip is sharing the good news, attributes and qualities of others. This form of Gossip includes the sharing of good information and reports. However, even though we hear good news from or about someone, it does not necessarily mean that we are entitled to share it. For example, it is not appropriate for a wife who has been told by her GP that she is pregnant, having told her best friend before her husband, for that best friend to then pass this good news on to the husband.

The purpose of this book is mainly primarily with negative Gossip, its ramifications, impact and destructive fallout. We will discuss how to avoid it, shut it down when it happens around us, as well as the steps that we can take to ensure that we do not become vehicles or the topics of Gossip.

All information that we hear should be treated with care and respect.

DEFINITIONS

It would be reasonable to assume that we have either been the subject of Gossip, shared Gossip with others listened to Gossip, or even, been the source of the story. If we have not been involved in these areas, then it could be that we have ourselves engaged in 'gossip.'

According to dictionary.com...
Gossip is the idle talking of rumours, true or false and especially about the personal or private affairs of others.

Gossip is the casual or unconstrained conversation or reports about other people, typically involving details that are not confirmed as being true.

According to Merriam Webster's Dictionary...

A gossip is a person who habitually reveals personal or sensational often intimate facts about others.

ENTER TALEBEARER

As gossip is generally passed on through the medium of a human being, an actual person. For the purposes of this book, our malicious gossip will be known as Talebearer.

By humanising and demonstrating that gossip is the activity of people, it will help us to recognise the damage done by us and/or others when engaging in gossip. As such, Talebearer is a pseudo-personality and will be referred to in the first person, Talebearer, so that you will recognise the personality of whom we speak.

Disclaimer
Talebearer is a purely fictitious character created by the author to humorously humanise individuals that engage in gossip.

This character is not intended to bear any likeness whatsoever or similarity to any person living or dead with a similar name.

PROLOGUE

As with all matters concerning human relationships, fragility and handling with care, is a must. Human relationships are very fragile elements with which human beings seek to live in peace and harmony with one another. All of the advice, suggestions and guidance given are to be executed with grace and humility.

Eliminating Gossip is not about putting people in their place and one-upmanship. Eliminating gossip is about knowing the dynamics of the human relationships that you are engaged in and living accordingly.

"A soft answer turns away wrath."

Always approach your encounters with Tail with grace and humility and watch how you change, talebearer changes, your environment and your communities change.

When challenging others, remember the GOLDEN RULE. Treat others as you would like them to treat you.

DAY 1

LET NO CORRUPT COMMUNICATION PROCEED FROM YOUR MOUTH

Let no corrupt communication proceed from your mouth, but that which is good to hearers. **The Bible**.

To corrupt something means to change it negatively from its original state of good into a less or worse state than its original condition.

When we allow corrupt communication from our mouths, it potentially changes (corrupts) the opinion of the hearer from a good or reasonable opinion into a detrimental opinion of the subject of the conversation. Having also the potential to change (corrupt) the hearer's opinion from a positive to a negative opinion of the person speaking.

Jewish Rabbis use the term 'Lashon Hora' to describe gossip. They call it 'evil speaking,' believing that evil speaking harms three people.

The person who is the subject of Gossip, because their character is being impugned and they are not present to defend themselves.

The person hearing Gossip, because they now have their opinion changed (corrupted) and choose to, rightly or wrongly, review the state of the original opinion they held of the person being spoken about. Especially if it becomes a lower opinion than they initially held.

The person speaking the Gossip, because they have exposed their heart to the hearer. The hearer may now hold a lower opinion of the speaker than they did in the first place. By gossiping or speaking evil, the gossip has impugned their own character.

The rabbi's teach that the only time it is permissible to share an evil truth, or what we might call a "bad report" about another person is, when not doing so will cause damage to the person that you plan to tell.

In other words, if I tell you that Mr X stole money from a shop, but you don't own the shop, I am speaking evil of Mr X, even if what I say is true. It would only be right for me to tell you about Mr X stealing from the shop if you are the shop owner and if you will personally suffer from it and if I don't tell you.

"A neighbourhood of voluntary spies surrounds every man."
Jane Austen

DAY 2

YOUR MOTHER CAN'T KNIT

Tell-tale tit,
Your mother can't knit,
Your nose is as long as a walking stick.

The reference to the nose being as long as a walking stick, is a description of the Gossip. That being, their nose is so long, that it is always getting stuck into other people's affairs and matters that do not concern them.

As children, we were forbidden to tell tales about other people. The telling of tales was forbidden in both home and school.

We were taught that telling tales is the character trait of a person that is not trustworthy. Along with not being able to trust the person, they could also be malicious and spiteful. We were also taught that telling tales has the potential to damage, hurt and cause injury to others. As we grew up, we learned not to tell tales and tell stories about other people. We also learned that usually the motivation behind the telling of tales being quite sordid: -

a) The person with the information, Talebearer, wishes to exert power, because they possess something you don't. Knowledge! Knowledge about another person.

b) Talebearers also seek to separate people who dwell in harmonious relationships of unity. Divide and rule, being two critical words to Talebearer.

c) Talebearers are insecure people, with a lot of emotional fears. For them, the passing on of information feeds their need to be esteemed as someone that possesses, what they wrongly believe, needed information.

d) Talebearer can be quite malicious, seeking to destroy relationships they perceive as a threat to them. As the Bible rightly asserts, "They will separate the best of friends."

e) Talebearer misuse's their intelligence, unwisely directing it into destructive practices. They can often be found to 'weaponise' information they possess about others to impugn them, their character and their status.

f) Talebearers wrongly believe that telling tales will improve their status in the eyes of others.

People that suffer from these kinds of motivations are to be pitied. They certainly need good and honest friends around them who know them well enough and are close enough to them to recognise these motivations and behaviours and will challenge them.

"Tale-bearers are as bad as the tale-makers."
Richard Brinsley Sheridan

DAY 3

TRUE, KIND, NECESSARY

There are two people to be challenged by hearing information about others.

The First person is Talebearer.
Ask Talebearer if what they have told you is *true*.
If they answer in the affirmative, ask them if they consider what they have told you is *kind*.
If they answer in the negative, then ask Talebearer if what they told you was necessary.

The second person to be challenged is yourself.
Having heard this information, ask yourself the same questions.

> ➤ **Is it true?**

If it is true, then you have opinions or facts.

If it is untrue, then you have been told lies and you therefore must disregard it. Even if it is true, it does not mean that you are free to repeat it.

> ➤ **Is it kind?**

If it is kind, then rejoice with those who rejoice.

If it is unkind, you must disregard this information as malicious gossip and are duty-bound not to repeat it...

> ➤ **Is it necessary?**

If it is necessary for you to know this information, then do what is correct, relevant and appropriate.

If it is not necessary for you to know this information, then disregard it.

"The three essential rules when speaking of others are: Is it true? Is it kind? Is it necessary?"
Author unknown

DAY 4

TOPIC OF JUICY GOSSIP

The Golden Rule of, "Treating others as you wish to be treated," may never be as accurate as when it comes to gossip and rumour-mongering.

To eliminate gossip from your life, imagine for a moment, if you dare, you have become aware that you are the topic of juicy gossip. Then, not only are you the subject of a juicy gossip, but also...

➤ The Gossip is circulating virally.

➤ It is untrue, scandalous, and slanderous.

➤ It has the potential to damage your reputation irreparably.

➤ It has the potential to damage personal and future relationships irreparably.

- You are truly powerless to stop the gossip and there is nothing you do to stop it circulating.

- You are utterly defenceless in the wake of all that is being spoken about you.

  Now!!!

- Imagine how you would feel.

- This too, is how others could feel when you partake of gossip about them.

"Cockroach has no business in a cock fight."
Jamaican Proverb

DAY 5

BREAKING CONFIDENCE

Have you ever had a friend tell you something in the strictest confidence? "Promise that you won't tell any anyone?" Do you notice that is more of an order than a request?

What they tell you might not even be gossip. It could be something true and your friend telling you, simply wants to share their heart with you about something that is important to them.

Don't break that confidence.

If information was given to you in confidence, then as a matter of integrity. You should never pass that information on to another person. Not your spouse, best friend, counsellor or mentor. Even if asked!

If the information that was given to you in confidence has the potential to harm another person, if not shared, then request permission of the person who shared that information with you, so that you can pass it on, where appropriate.

For example, if someone tells you in confidence that they are employing the services of a child-minder to take care of their home and children whilst they go out to work. It is however, a commonly known fact that the person they are about to employ is a known thief with a history of preying on vulnerable children, you are of course obligated to reveal what you know about the potential cleaner.

"I would not tell you if I was hungry."
The Bible

DAY 6

SLANDER

Is what you have been told, slanderous?

If the answer to this question is, "Yes," then ensure that you exercise great caution and certainly a massive dose of self-control and discipline before repeating it to another, or you may find yourself in the middle of a very expensive lawsuit.

Slander does not necessarily have to be lies about another person. Even if something is, *'true,'* the repetition of it can be considered slanderous; especially if the motivation behind its repetition is to injure the reputation and the character of the person being spoken about. In these instances, it's not necessarily *what* is said but the *way* it is said that can cause damage.

"Your tongue says more about you when it blabs about other people."
Richelle E. Goodrich,

GOSSIP IS ILLEGAL

The Guardian online newspaper reported in 2019, that the Mayor of Binalonan, passed an 'anti-Gossip' ordinance due to the escalating Gossip over many civil issues that were getting out of control.

The Guardian reports as follows:
The anti-Gossip ordinance was passed by the Binalonan mayor, Ramon Guico III, after several disputes fuelled by Gossip had got "so severe", with multiple parties involved, that the local council had to intervene.

"There are many types of Gossip, but most Gossip case are about conflict around property, money, relationships and the like," Guico told the Guardian. "This ordinance is to remind people that everything we say is our responsibility as individuals and as residents of this municipality. In addition, we want to show other towns that Binalonan has good people; it is a good and safe place to stay."[1]

For those caught fuelling the rumour mill or peddling salacious stories in Binalonan, the punishment for a first-time offender is a fine of 200 pesos (£3) and three hours of community service, picking up rubbish. Repeat offenders will face a fine of up to £15 and eight hours' community service. They however, confirmed that some residents had already been caught and punished under the new law and it had succeeded in reducing local disputes.

The ban was first imposed on the Capas neighbourhood of the municipality of Binalonan, but proved so successful that it has been extended to seven villages in the district. "Banning Gossip is our way of improving the quality of life in our town," said Guico. "A Gossip-less town is more fruitful because I believe people have better things to do than talk negatively about others."

---

[1] https://www.theguardian.com/world/2019/may/01/have-you-heard-about-the-philippine-mayor-who-banned-Gossip

DAY 7

STRAIGHT FROM THE HORSE'S MOUTH

Offer Talebearer of the opportunity to repeat the information they have a shared with you, in front of the person who told it to them, or that the gossip is about.

On occasions when an individual has shared something with me about another person, and it is hugely detrimental, I have often offered the opportunity for us both to visit the person concerned and discuss the matter in front of them.

This will usually shutdown any form of gossip, and Talebearer will refrain from wanting to bring gossip to your ears.

Unless what I hear comes from a proven, trustworthy and honourable character, or straight from the horse's mouth, I generally take it with a pinch of salt.

I will certainly not pass it on. I subsequently find that Talebearer ends up refraining from coming to me with their nasty news.

"Never engage in gossip, it kills your soul, and wounds another's heart."
Steven Aitchison

DAY 8

WE ARE OUR BROTHERS KEEPER

If Talebearer brings news to you of something that is extremely serious, don't be afraid to ask questions to ascertain facts. It may be that something needs to be done with the information you are hearing, especially if a serious crime may have been committed.

Invite Talebearer to name the source of the information. You may well find, that upon requesting the source, Talebearer is reluctant to name the source and even go as far as withdrawing or recanting the information.

If Talebearer is reluctant to reveal the source. It could mean that the information is in fact doubtful, and certainly cannot be confirmed. Neither is it to be trusted.

This was my experience many years ago. I was told a snippet of news that, if true, would certainly have meant a jail sentence for the person concerned.

I asked Talebearer to tell me the source of this information. Needless to say they were quite reluctant and even went as far as to confess that it might not even be true.

Firstly, I challenge their misplaced boldness in the repeating of information they were not even sure was accurate.

Secondly, I strongly encouraged them not to pass on this information to anyone else, especially in the light of the fact they were not even sure that it could be true.

Thirdly, I suggested that they return to all the people they had already shared this information with. They were to inform them that they, Talebearer, could not confirm the truthfulness of what had been said and they were to dismiss it as idle gossip.

Of course, Talebearer was not enamoured with my suggestions, but clearly felt they had no option, especially as they could not confirm the accuracy of that piece of misinformation.

Subsequently, it was discovered that the said piece of news was indeed idle and malicious gossip. Thankfully it had been stopped in its tracks, and no harm had been done.

We may find this a difficult conversation to have. However, this course of action and conversation is essential if we are going to eliminate gossip and spare an innocent party from unnecessary heartache.

Who knows? You could find yourself very grateful to a person who took this course of action on your behalf, and spared you from a ruined reputation. Their intervention will have prevented inaccurate news and gossip being spread about you.

We are our brother's keeper!

"Isn't it silly to think that tearing someone else down builds you up?"
Sean Covey

DAY 9

WHY ARE YOU SAYING THIS TO ME?

For those who know me well, they are familiar with me constantly asking questions. The reason that I asked questions is so that I can learn, understand and empathise

In the event that an individual is telling me information, I find that I need to understand why I am being told the said information, so that I'm able to process it into a relevant context.
I therefore often ask individuals questions about what they are saying,

I ask, "Why are you saying this to me?

I also ask, "Should you be telling me this?"

"Why are you sharing this with me?" Could be the very challenge Talebearer needs to inspect their own motives, as to why they are indeed sharing this information with you.

Answers can vary from...

> "Well, I just thought I'd pass it on."

> "I think you ought to know." Which case it may not be Gossip but need-to-know information.

> "I just want them to look bad."

> "They are always talking about me and others."

One reply often quoted is,
> "Well, so that you can pray intelligently about it."

Yeah right! As though God isn't intelligent enough to know about the issue already.

Talebearer has been known to say to everyone that they share this piece of information with...,

> ➤ "I know you that won't tell anyone."

Yet, eventually, many people will know the information passed on by at least one of the people, "Who would never tell anybody."

"You just know that someone loves your cos your name is safe in their mouth."
Billy Aged 4

DAY 10

PERMISSION AND HAPPY

Ask Talebearer if they have permission to be sharing this news with you. I usually interrupt Talebearer with, "Excuse me, but do you have So and So's express permission to be telling me this news?"

Talebearers are not always liars. On the contrary, they may well be very truthful individuals. Yet, they will be embarrassed at this question. They will be honest about whether they have So and So's permission to be sharing.

If they answer in the negative, that is generally a good place to stop them passing on any more information. Something like, "Well, thank you for your honesty, in that case, you had better not tell me anymore."

Sometimes people don't want you to know something about them, simply because they don't. Individuals have their own reasons for retaining certain information about themselves. They have the right to their privacy and you don't have to know everything about them.

It is not uncommon for Gossips to tell you the latest information about another, whether good or bad. It's not even always nasty news. It may simply be something that they/you, simply don't need to know. The person who is the topic of Gossip would not want you to know for no other reason than they, 'just don't.'

When confronted with such a situation, interrupt Talebearer with, "Excuse me, but would So and So be happy if they knew you were sharing this information about them with me."

Talebearer will be embarrassed and confess that So and So may indeed, not be happy with this information being shared.

Again, something like, "Well, thank you for your honesty. In that case, you best not tell me anymore." This usually works and Talebearer will not continue with the conversation.

These simple questions will eliminate any questionable motives and is a gentle and kind way of letting Talebearer down.

"Gossip, as usual, was one-third right and two-thirds wrong."
L.M. Montgomery

DAY 11

FAULT FINDING

We all have faults, weaknesses and character flaws. None of us are perfect, as much as we do like to think that we might be.

Try to avoid discussing with another person the faults, defects and weaknesses that you observe in an individual, especially if the individual that you observe the faults in, have nothing to do with you.

Do not let another individual discuss with you faults, defects and weaknesses of another. Again, especially if the person or their flaws have nothing to do with your life purpose and business.

We are all on a journey and most fair-minded people are sincerely seeking to work on, correct and eliminate their flaws and defects.

How about we all believe the best about one another and believe that each one of us is making our own individual effort and endeavouring to become better individuals and even better versions of ourselves.

"Never listen to talk about the weaknesses of others. If someone complains of another, you can tell them humbly, to say nothing of it to you."
St John of the Cross

DAY 12

STOP THEM IN THEIR TRACKS

It may be that you know that you have heard too much already.

Be bold and interrupt and state, "As So and So is not present, and I would rather not listen to what you have to say." This may seem like a difficult thing to do or say, but if you have to say it often enough, you will soon feel comfortable saying it and know it is the right thing to do.

Stop them in their tracks!

Bold I know, however, it always works!

For some people it's the only way!

"Shut the Gossip of men as much as possible."
Thomas a Kempis

FAST FACTS ABOUT GOSSIP

Everyone Gossips. Gossip is ubiquitous. Researchers noted in the paper published in the Social Psychological and Personality Science journal, that: -

- ➢ Less educated people don't Gossip more than wealthier, better-educated ones.

- ➢ Extroverts Gossip far more frequently than introverts while women gossip more than men but only in neutral, information-sharing gossip.

- ➢ The findings showed that about 14 per cent of participants' conversations were gossiping, for just under an hour in 16 waking hours.

- ➢ Almost three quarters of Gossip was neutral, and negative gossip (604 instances) was twice as prevalent as positive (376).

➤ Gossip overwhelmingly was about an acquaintance and not a celebrity, with a comparison of 3,292 samples vs. 369."[2]

---

[2] This study reveals some psychological facts about Gossiping - Gossip mongering | The Economic Times (indiatimes.com)

DAY 13

STOP!

THEY ARE NOT HERE.

Where appropriate, inform Talebearer that you prefer not to listen to information about any person that is not present.

This might be challenging as sometimes the subject of their conversation can never be present. Maybe because of geographical location, personal circumstances, or they might even be dead.

However, when someone is not present to defend themselves or correct misinformation, you may need to do this on their behalf.

Stating something like "Excuse me, but So and So is not here to put their side of the situation. Therefore, I'm sure you will agree, that it might be prudent for us to refrain from discussing this matter any further."

This will usually silence Talebearer and you have done it in a kindly manner.

"If you can't find something good to say, zip your lip.."
George Aitchison

DAY 14

LA LA LA

I'M NOT LISTENING

Talebearer can be a thick-skinned individual who can be extremely persistent despite your protestations. They may well insist that you listen to what they have to say.

When all else fails, let Talebearer know that you will not listen and stick your fingers in your ears and shout, "La, la, la, la, la I'm not listening."

It works – trust me!

"If there is anything more annoying in the world than having people talk about you, it is certainly having no one talk about you."
Oscar Wilde

DAY 15

CHALLENGE, CHALLENGE, CHALLENGE

Challenges such as...

➤ "I don't believe that is true at all."

➤ "How do you know that what you are saying is true?"

➤ "How many people have you told this information to?"

➤ "If that is true, I think you should talk straightaway to So and So Let them know this is being said about them. They need to put it right, if it is not true."

➤ "You have told me this and as I don't know whether it is true or not, so I am not going to repeat this to anyone else."

Again, you have communicated to Talebearer in a polite yet firm way that you are not interested in their Gossip.

"If you can't write it, sign it, then don't say it."
George Aitchison

DAY 16

EMPATHISE AND SYMPATHISE

When Talebearer arrives with their news about So and So, empathise and sympathise with So and So

Suggested responses could be something like...

> "So and So may have been having a bad day, may have suffered a bereavement coming through a period of illness."

> "Oh dear, I'm very sorry to hear you say that about So and So Maybe they are having a rough time right now. Give them grace and a bit of slack, they may need our support."

> "It's a pity that you have said that about So and So, because they are usually a real

darling, which makes me think that things must be tough for them right now."

➤ "There could be another angle on what you are saying. Maybe it's a good idea to get all the facts before forming a firm judgement."

➤ "Are you sure about that? I would love to think that what you're saying is not true."

➤ "Are you able to check that with (name of person being gossiped about) directly so that you can be sure of your facts? It would be awful if you repeated it and then found out it was misinformation that you were sharing"

Talebearer will interpret your comments as, "I will not be in agreement with you today."

"Women shouldn't judge each other's lives, if we haven't been through one another's fires."
Lisa Taddeo,

DAY 17

DEFEND THEIR HONOUR

When Talebearer gossips about a person, and especially if you know them, defend the honour of that person. Everybody has good qualities. Even those who are perceived as difficult, there can always be found something good about them.

When Talebearer denigrates another individual, share good qualities of that individual. You do not have to divulge sensitive information about them. You can explain positive graces you observed in that individual's life.

- ➤ "In my experience, I always find So and So to be honest, hard-working and a good .... whatever is appropriate.

- ➤ "I see great qualities in So and So They are a very empathetic and compassionate person."

- ➤ "Really? I observe patience and kindness in them, so I am very surprised to hear you speak like this about them."

- ➤ "What you say is interesting because whenever I have met them, I have always found them to be polite, courteous, generous, kind and warm-hearted."

You are of course free to use your own statements, so long as they are honest and relevant to that setting.

When you become known as a person that only sees and speaks the best of others, Talebearer will think twice before bringing their tales to you.

"It's only Gossip if you repeat it.
Until then, it's gathering information."
Mercedes Lackey

DAY 18

ALWAYS ASSUME CONFIDENTIALITY

We have all had the following said to us, or even said it ourselves to others. "I am saying this to you in the strictest confidence. Promise me that you will not repeat this to another living soul." This is often said, because we know that all of us as humans share information with others. Sometimes it is intentional. Most times it is unintentional. We can, if not careful, habitually repeat and share information with others, many times, without even thinking about it.

A simple rule to train and adopt for yourself, to ensure that you do not even accidentally pass on information that you have heard, is to, *'automatically assume confidentiality'.*

I have a personal rule, that whatever I have been told, regardless of whether I have been sworn to secrecy or not, I automatically assume confidentiality. I do this because, when I am given information, it is not usually precipitated or concluded with the caveat, "Okay, now Elaine, you are free to go and tell everybody what you know." It is not merely 'clergy confidentiality,' that I observed. For me, it is about honour and personal integrity in how I handle information.

When an individual tells you something, ask yourself this one question. "Did they give me permission to repeat what they have just said to everybody that I meet?" It would be a fair guess to say that 10 times out of 10 times they did not say, "There you go, now I have told you, you can now repeat it to the four winds."

In the absence of being given permission to repeat, it would be most reasonable to assume that what has been told to you is not for repeating. You can therefore assume that *it is confidential*.

"Those who Gossip to you will eventually Gossip about you. "
Author unknown

GOSSIP AS EVIDENCE OF

CULTURAL LEARNING

Some scholars view gossip as evidence of cultural learning, offering teachable moments and providing people examples of what's socially acceptable — and what's not.

For example, if there's someone who cheats a lot in a community or social circle and people start to talk about that person in a negative way, the collective criticism should warn others of the consequences of cheating. And as word near-inevitably trickles back to source of said gossip, it can "serve to keep people in check, morally speaking,"[3]

"He who criticises, may well be doing so to hide their own faults."
George Aitchison

---

[3] https://time.com/5680457/why-do-people-gossip/

DAY 19

NEVER SWEAR

You may have been told information that could include the breaking of the law or putting the lives of others at risk.

You may hear something that you absolutely know that you cannot in any circumstances permanently keep confidential.

The law may have been broken and you have been told information that will solve the crime, imprison the culprit and protect the innocent. In those circumstances, it is nearly always impossible to keep information confidential.

In the event that an individual is telling you information and seeking your confidence. The best response to their plea of confidentiality, is to inform them that before they tell you anything, if what they are about to say involves breaking the law, hurting themselves or others, then you may be obliged to repeat that information to the necessary authorities.

You are not saying that you will not keep it confidential. You are merely advising that you may have to repeat it if the criteria you have laid out is breached. That way, you have given the individual the information they need to make an informed decision as to whether they continue telling you what they were about to say.

"Never judge someone's character based on the words of another. Instead, study the motives behind the words of the person casting the bad judgement."
Suzy Kassem

DAY 20

SECOND-HAND IS ALWAYS CHEAPER

'Brand new' clothes, usually have a 'brand new' price-tag on them. However, when those clothes have been worn for some time they depreciate in value and have a lesser value than when brand new.

When you hear news that is second-hand, that too may be worn and depreciated in value. Valuable, truths and facts can be lost, misinterpreted, reinterpreted, embellished thus making it of lesser value than when the information was brand new.

Try to form the habit, of when Talebearer shares snippets of information with you, by asking questions like: -

> ➤ "Did you *hear* them say those exact words yourself – or was it second-hand?"

- ➢ "Did you *see/hear* that event with your own eyes/ears or is it second-hand because another person told you?"

- ➢ "Were you there when it was said/ happened?"

By asking searching and probing questions you can eliminate Gossip. You are communicating to Talebearer that you are not simply prepared to accept a statement that they say to you because it is them that said it and especially if it is second-hand.

Just like second-hand goods being cheaper than when they are brand new. Second-hand information can also be cheapened, by embellishments, additions, subtractions and distortion of facts.

"You mouth will always amplify your heart."
Hugh Osgood

DAY 21

EXIT

You may find yourself in a setting where salacious Gossip is being dispensed and you can do nothing, say nothing to protect those being spoken about. You also observe that the situation is escalating and getting out of hand. However, _speaking up_ and _speaking out_ on this occasion, is not an option!

Therefore, a polite and friendly, "Excuse me please," and then walking away, without making a fuss of your exit, is sufficient.

You may well be asked later on, if you are okay and why you excused yourself. If you feel comfortable in doing so, you can say that you were not comfortable with the topic of conversation at that precise moment, and so as not to listen or participate, you chose to excuse yourself.

I have, from time to time found myself in the position where I do not like or appreciate the conversation; and been powerless to challenge or change the subject.

I have simply said, "Please excuse me" and walked away.

"A perverse man stirs up dissension and a talebearer separates close friends."
The Bible

DAY 22

CHANGE THE SUBJECT

Talebearer, as we have discussed, can be quite insecure. We do not want to be adding to their sense of insecurity by sounding judgemental and disapproving.

A swift course of action can be to change the subject from the person who is the topic of conversation. This can be done in a light-hearted, gentle yet firm manner by making statements like...

> ➤ "Hey, there are more interesting topics we can be talking about, what about the... (Name yours or their favourite topic)."

> ➤ Yes, okay, it's easy to talk about their faults and misgivings, (or whatever the subject is) let's see if between us we can identify their top 10 good qualities and traits about them.

> "I know that, So and So is probably a juicy piece of Gossip right now, but what about that cruise you went on, your project, or something else relevant. Tell me about that."

Done in this way, which is loving and kind, you are not casting aspersions upon Talebearer and they will not feel that they are being judged out of hand.

You will have stopped the topic in its tracks, and you will have caused Talebearer to consider their own motivation and actions.

A sure winner!

"To the person who wishes to find fault. THAT is 'your' fault."
George Aitchison

DAY 23

I AM NOT IN A POSITION TO SAY

The character of Talebearer can at times be wrapped up with delusions and self-deceptions. They like the ill-perceived sense of power they think that they possess. They oftentimes also believe that they possess the right to extract information from others.

When I am questioned about a matter and Talebearer wants me to pass on information that they either think I have, or know that I have. I have a simple and stock reply. It is quite a bold statement. It is not a lie. It is the truth.

I state to Talebearer, "I am not in position to say."

If I do know the answer to what they are asking.
> ➤ The truth is, I could discuss this with you, if I wanted to. I don't want to.

Therefore, "I am not in position to say."
➤ The truth is, I could discuss it this with you, if I had permission. I don't have permission.
"Therefore, "I am not in position to say."

➤ The truth is, I do not wish to discuss it with you. I will not discuss it with you. Therefore, "I am not in position to say."

If I don't know the answer to what they're asking.
➤ The truth is, I do not have the information that you are seeking to pry out of me.
Therefore, "I am not in position to say."

Both are true. I cannot say and I will not say. I choose not to make a full explanation of these points to Talebearer, as I do believe I am required to be accountable to them.

"He who goes about as a Gossip reveals secrets; therefore, do not associate with one who flatters with his lips."
The Bible

DAY 24

CONFESS VULNERABILITIES

If you want to stop people from sharing their tales, rumours and general Gossip about others with you, you may consider confessing any previous vulnerability that you may have had in this area. Inform them that you don't want to re-engage in that nasty habit.

You may say something like, "You know, I've had a problem in the past with gossip, listening to and passing on other people's information and it caused me problems. I'd rather not be caught in that position again. I'd be really grateful if you didn't share any more information about that with me."

Nobody is going to get offended or argue with you or challenge you when you make such humble, loving and caring statement as that.

They, however, may be slightly embarrassed, or even convicted themselves

At the same time, you have lovingly encouraged Talebearer to reconsider their own personal habit.

"It isn't what they say about you, it's what they whisper."
Errol Flynn

EFFECTS OF GOSSIP IN THE BRAIN

Peng et al. (2015) examined brain imaging of men and women as they listened to positive and negative gossip about themselves and celebrities. People who heard either positive or negative gossip about themselves showed more activity in the prefrontal cortex of their brains, which helps people navigate complex social behaviours. This reaction also occurred when the participants heard negative gossip in general. This research demonstrates that people want to fit in socially, and they also want others to see them in a positive light.

Peng et al. (2015) also found that the caudate nucleus, the reward centre in the brain, activated in response to negative gossip about celebrities, which demonstrates how salacious celebrity scandals pique people's interest. Predictably, the study showed that people felt happier when they heard positive gossip about themselves and felt more agitated when they heard negative gossip about themselves.

Gossiping is rewarded, so people will continue to gossip as long as they do not hear anything negative about themselves. It is OK to talk negatively about others, but do not say anything bad about me.

People like to gossip. Gossip is information shared about an absent third party. Gossip differs from the human tendency to talk about other people in that gossip tends to focus on negative information to demean the target. If the information being talked about were positive, it would be labelled praise or envy.

Gossip typically centres on the negative aspects of a person's personal appearance, personal achievements, or personal behaviours.

A less benign form of gossip is when people discuss information about celebrities or other people highlighted in tabloids or social media.

DAY 25

CAN I REPEAT THIS?

Not everything that you hear is wicked Gossip about another person.

To act in complete integrity regarding news or information that is given to you, it is good practice to ask the news giver, if it is OK to share this news with spouse or another person.

"Is this news OK to repeat?" or something similar.

When you then share this news, you can then say I do have permission to share this.

In asking for permission to repeat and then explaining to your listeners that you have (a) asked for and (b) received permission to repeat, you model to your listener that you are not repeating news inappropriately. You also model to them a better way of handling other people's information.

Often times, people can think that by not saying names, places and anonymising the person they are talking about, that they are not breaking a confidence. THEY ARE!

How many times have you heard others speak of another in anonymous terms, yet you know exactly who they are talking about?

It has been suggested that there are only six degrees of separation between all people. Even anonymising the information, you can be assured that out of every seven or eight people that you tell, someone will know the person of whom you speak.

If you do wish to repeat information, even anonymously, always obtain permission.

"I would not tell them what I had for breakfast."
Author Unknown

DAY 26

PRIVATE LIFE

Private life, is so-called free good reason.

If you do not want to become the centre of unwanted and salacious misinformation and Gossip, then a good discipline and course of action is to keep your 'private life, *private.*'

In the absence of information, rumour mongers will leave you alone.

However, if you choose to share segments of sensitive information about your private life in general conversation, then do not be surprised if people fill in the gaps and make up the rest.

"Every man is surrounded by a neighbourhood of voluntary spies."
Jane Austen

DAY 27

MIND YOUR Ps AND Qs

Mind your Ps and Qs in British culture means to 'mind your manners.' Ps and Qs is an important matter where Gossip is concerned.

In the event of Talebearer approaching you and asking your opinion about another person, a few simple tips to deal with their question, is to say something like ...

> "It's not good manners to talk about people that are not present."

> "Why do you want to know?" If there truly is a valid reason and it is not Gossip, then it could be important that you state, not your opinion, but what you know to be true.

> "Why do you want to know?" If it is because they are 'just' interested, you can inform

them that your opinion of the individual concerned is your sacred and private affair.

➤ "Why, what is your opinion of them?" If Talebearer shares a good report about the person and you agree, then only if you feel it's appropriate and are comfortable, you may wish to share your opinion. Ensure that in sharing, your opinion is positive and uplifting about the person.

➤ If your opinion is not positive but negative, you then need to exercise self-control and discipline, stating that your opinion of about that individual is your sacred and private affair.

➤ You may say, "I don't have an opinion."

"In small towns, news travels at the speed of boredom."
Carlos Ruiz Zafón

DAY 28

MIND YOUR OWN BUSINESS

Gossip, in general has very little to do with our individual lives, focus, ambitions, life purpose and relationships.

Usually, we don't Gossip, intentionally about others. Yet, if we are not careful, when asked an opinion about an individual and we give it, that opinion can be shared to a third, fourth, fifth and even twentieth party. Unwittingly, your opinion has contributed to a rumour about that person. Even though you had no intention of being the source of a rumour about that person.

Be careful with the words that you speak, ensuring that you are not, even unintentionally starting a rumour yourself

To ensure that you do not get entangled in Gossip and unnecessary chat, set the personal boundary of *minding your own business*.

When hearing others gossip about a particular topic or person. A simple statement like, "Actually, this is nothing to do with me and is not going to impact my life in anyway, so I'd rather not know. Thank you."

Again you have communicated in a firm yet polite manner that you are not interested and will not contribute or partake in Gossip.

"Although every rumour has a grain of truth, I've found that the worst Gossip usually starts with something harmless."
Kathleen O'Dell,

DAY 29

CAN'T LISTEN - WON'T LISTEN

➤ When you do these things you will become known as a person who *will not listen* to *Gossip*

➤ When you do these things, you will become as known as a person who will not *spread Gossip*

➤ When you do these things, people will know that they *cannot come to you with their Gossip*

➤ When you do these things, people will know that they *cannot come to you for Gossip*

"A boomerang returns to the person who throws it. But first, while moving in a circle, it hits its target. So does Gossip."
Vera Nazarian

DAY 30

CHOICES

You reached the end of this book

CONGRATULATIONS!

I trust that you will have read, being inspired and recognised that you do not have a Gossip problem. On the other hand, you may feel concerned about the negative gossip that you have engaged in. If so, the invitation at this point, is to repent and tell God that you are sorry for Gossiping.

It would be unwise to go to the individual/s you have Gossiped about and confess your crimes against them. Doing so, could be destructive to your relationship with them and others. The best thing to do is, having repented and apologised to God, is to ensure that you do not continue to engage in Gossip.

If, on the other hand, you and the party concerned both recognise the harm caused by your words. As a matter of honour to them, a good discipline for yourself and personal integrity;*[4] the decent thing to do, is to make a full and unreserved apology.

Something like... "I have said some very unkind things about you.   I was wrong and I wish to offer my unreserved apology. I ask for your forgiveness. Please will/can you forgive me?" Then move on.

Best option, is not to send an email or text message. Have a face-to-face. If possible, there are plenty of alternatives, Zoom, WhatsApp.

If the person is no longer alive, forgive yourself and move on.

---

[4] *For more information on integrity, please read in this series, "31 Days to Developing Personal Integrity." Developing Personal Integrity is a modules taught in great detail on the Practical Christian Ministry Course at Every Nation Bible School UK – info@enbs.co.uk

"Without wood fire goes out; without Gossip quarrel dies down."
The Bible

DAY 31

WELL DONE!

YOU MADE IT TO DAY 31

There are no more instructions to follow.

Keep up the good work and remind yourself of any key points that have been useful and helpful to you.

Congratulations as you pursue and continue a gossip free' lifestyle.

God bless you!

ABOUT THE AUTHOR

Elaine Roberts is married to Peter. Their two children James and Sarah are in heaven.

Elaine has been in full-time Christian ministry for over 30 years. She is an apostolic leader and founder of World Mandate Ministries and Every Nation Bible School UK based in Northampton, England.

Along with Peter and their loyal, dedicated, committed and hard-working team, World Mandate Ministries have equipped literally thousands and thousands of individuals preparing them to fulfil vocational service and ministry both within and outside of the church.

Elaine loves people and embraces people in her heart and life, regardless of their status, treating all with equal honour and respect.

Elaine has travelled to over 25 nations preaching the Gospel of Jesus Christ and equipping God's people to serve Him in their God ordained callings.

The fruit of Elaine's extensive leadership experience is directed into coaching and mentoring leaders and individuals, particularly those seeking direction in their life and ministry.

Elaine is an ordained minister with Churches in Communities, International, (CIC). She has earned a Masters in Applied Theology, Diploma in Coaching and Mentoring, and is also a qualified Internal Quality Assurer.

As a conference speaker, Elaine inspires and ministers with Biblical wisdom, Godly confidence and spiritual authority to release to those who are truly seeking to make an impact in their communities and leave a lasting legacy to the world.

If you wish, Elaine to speak at your conference, seminar or church meeting then please feel free to contact her on info@godsmandate.org

31 DAY SERIES

31 Days of powerful, life changing insights for spirit, soul, body and character transformation

31 Day Series: is a dynamic and empowering series on personal development and self-improvement.

31 Day Series: the contents and guidance given in the have been applied and observed by the author and many others.

31 Day Series: encourages and transforms readers from mediocrity to excellence.

31 Day Series: empowers readers to cultivating and developing outstanding and first-class character traits.

31 Days has stood the test of time, producing positive fruit in the lives of those who have observed and applied the guidance given.

MORE TO COME IN THE

31 DAYS SERIES...

The purpose of this growing 31 Days series of powerful and life changing books are to inspire individuals to reach for greater heights in personal, spiritual and character development.

Experienced, learned and applied wisdom will be shared, enabling and empowering individuals to become even better versions of themselves.

More titles are currently in the pipeline and will soon be available on Amazon.

31 Days to Developing Personal Integrity

31 Days to Becoming a Better Wife

More titles in the 31 Days series coming soon...

IF YOU WISH TO KNOW MORE

WORLD MANDATE MINISTRIES

www.godsmandate.org

info@godsmandate.org

Tel: +44 1604 759 039

EVERY NATION BIBLE SCHOOL UK

www.enbs.co.uk

info@enbs.co.uk

Tel: +44 1604 759 039

Printed in Great Britain
by Amazon